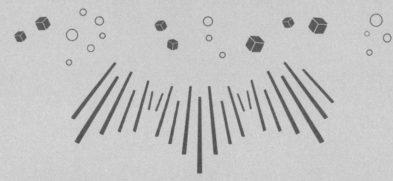

# CLASSIC &
# CONTEMPORARY
# COCKTAILS

An Hachette UK Company
www.hachette.co.uk

First published in Great Britain in 2018 by Hamlyn,
an imprint of Octopus Publishing Group Ltd
Carmelite House, 50 Victoria Embankment, London EC4Y 0DZ
www.octopusbooks.co.uk

ISBN 978-0-75373-342-4

A CIP catalogue record for this book is available from the British Library

Printed and bound in China

10 9 8 7 6 5 4 3 2 1

Publisher: Lucy Pessell
Designer: Lisa Layton
Editor: Sarah Vaughan
Production Manager: Caroline Alberti
Cover and interior motifs created by: Abhimanyu Bose, LSE Designs, Magicon,
Valeriy, Wuppdidu, Waiyi Fung. All from *The Noun Project*.

The measure that has been used in the recipes is based on a bar jigger, which is 25 ml (1 fl oz).
If preferred, a different volume can be used, providing the proportions are kept constant within a
drink and suitable adjustments are made to spoon measurements, where they occur.

Standard level spoon measurements are used in all recipes.
1 tablespoon = one 15 ml spoon
1 teaspoon = one 5 ml spoon

This book contains cocktails made with raw or lightly cooked eggs. It is prudent for more vulnerable
people to avoid uncooked or lightly cooked cocktails made with eggs.

Some of this material previously appeared in *Hamlyn All Colour Cookery: 200 Classic Cocktails* and
*501 Must-Drink Cocktails*.

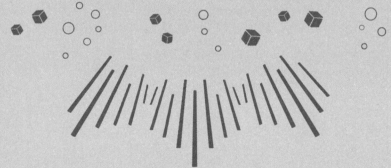

# CLASSIC &
# CONTEMPORARY
# COCKTAILS

hamlyn

# CONTENTS

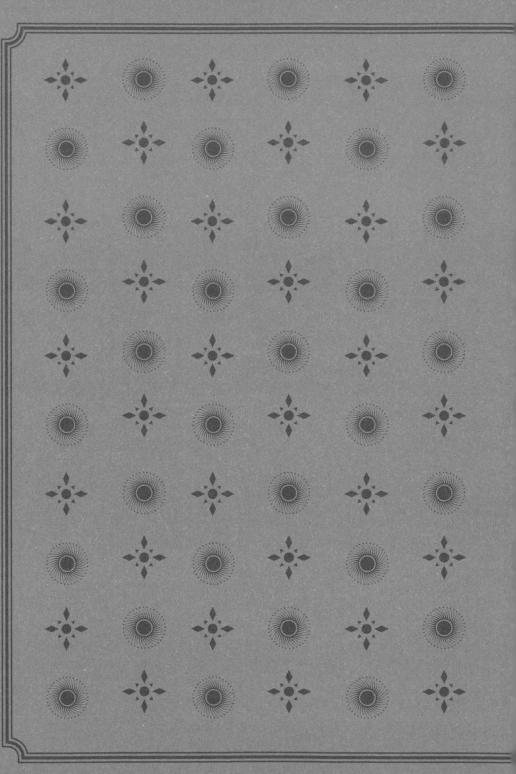

# A BRIEF HISTORY OF COCKTAILS & SOME FAVOURITE TIPPLES

# COCKTAILS

The origin of the word 'COCKTAIL' is widely disputed.

Initially used to describe the docked tails of horses that were not thoroughbred (which hasn't much to do with a Singapore Sling), the alleged first definition of a 'cocktail' appeared in New York's *The Balance and Columbian Repository*. In response to the question 'What is a cocktail?' the editor replied: 'it is a stimulating liquor, composed of spirits of any kind, sugar, water and bitters... in as much as it renders the heart stout and bold, at the same time that it fuddles the head... because a person, having swallowed a glass of it, is ready to swallow anything else.' Which sounds a little more like it.

However it began, this delightful act of mixing varying amounts of spirits, sugar and bitters has evolved, after decades of fine crafting, experimentation and even 13 years of prohibition in the United States, into the 'cocktail' we know and love. Each one a masterpiece. Each one to be made just right for you.

In the century since Harry Craddock concocted the Corpse Reviver and the White Lady, James Bond has insisted on breaking the number 1 rule to not shake a Martini every time he goes to the bar, and *Sex and the City* has introduced a whole new generation of drinkers to the very pink, very fabulous, Cosmopolitan cocktail. And the idea it can be paired with a burger and fries. Which is fine by us.

Go forth and make yours a Martini. Or a French Afternoon at gin o'clock on a mizzly Monday morning.

# GIN

GIN is (usually) a clear spirit distilled from grain or malt and then flavoured with juniper berries and other botanical products.

The name Gin is derived from the French *genièvre,* or the Dutch *jenever* – both meaning 'juniper' (and both harder to pronounce than the Latin 'juniperus').

Hailing from early 17th century Holland, Gin was initially produced as a medicine rather than a spirit, to which juniper was added only to make it more palatable. Thank you, Medicine.

Gin has come a long way since then. Once given to soothe stomach complaints and warm troops at war, it has established itself as one of the most popular spirits and is known to alleviate the downs (and boost the ups) of the head and heart, and warm troops at the bar.

It's at the heart of celebrated classic cocktails such as the Martini, Singapore Sling, Negroni and Tom Collins (the list is, thankfully, endless), and this oh-so versatile spirit deserves the role of 'truly magic ingredient number one' in a host of modern twists and contemporary concoctions.

# PROSECCO

**PROSECCO** is an Italian sparkling (spumante) or semi-sparkling (frizzante) white wine.

Originally made with the 'Glera' grape, and hailing from the Italian village of Prosecco near Trieste, Prosecco as we know it is now produced in nine provinces, and often from a blend of grapes. It has officially been recognised as 'the best thing ever' and has been protected by DOC and DOCG status.

Its popularity in the last decade has rocketed and the idea that Prosecco is simply Champagne's poor cousin is on the wane. Prosecco, with its light and spritzy bubbles is often fruitier and more floral than Champagne, and just happens to be cheaper as its aging time is a fraction of that of Champagne's: tank-aged rather than bottle-aged.

Prosecco is at the effervescent heart of the Bellini, and is the magic ingredient in the Italian Spritz recipe but it has a place in every cocktail that calls for bubbles.

In here you'll find some classic 'Champagne' cocktails dating back to times before we'd even heard of Prosecco (imagine! The Dark Ages!), some modern twists and some 'skip the soda and bring on the bubbles' creations.

# VODKA

**VODKA** is a clear spirit distilled from either fermented grains, potatoes (yes really), or fruit.

It hails from Russia and Eastern Europe, although specifically where is the subject of ~~heated argument~~ lively debate, with both Poland and Russia claiming vodka as their own brilliant idea (although Poland have court documents to prove it's theirs, so there). These days, the 'vodka belt' extends from Iceland in the west and the far reaches of Russia in the east, buckling-in Scandinavia, the Baltic states, Poland, Belarus and Ukraine as it goes on its belty way.

Vodka is traditionally drunk neat - a testament to its crisp, clean taste - but flavouring crept in over the centuries (originally to mask the unfortunate 'essence of homemadeness' that finds its way into many a popluar spirit made in the shed). It's now the bracing backbone of many a cocktail and pairs well with any flavour, from sweet to savoury and dry to spicy.  Whether pairing it improves the taste of the vodka, or vodka improves the taste of the pairing, is a matter of personal opinion although vodka improving the taste of everything else would be the correct opinion.

Best of all, it is the active ingredient in the only known cure for a hangover. Thanks to the Bloody Mary, we need not fear a few rounds with the bloomin' marvellous Cosmopolitan or Long Island Iced Tea.
Cheers to Good Health!

# WHISKY

**WHISKY**, or **WHISKEY**, is a caramel to deep brown spirit made from fermented grains such as rye and barley, and is aged in wooden barrels.

Whisky is as old as the hills. Probably the hills of Ireland but we can't be quite sure so we'll stick with 'hills'.

'Whisky' is an anglicization of the Gaelic 'water of life', from the Latin 'aqua vitae'. Had the people in charge of translation back then known it by its other name, 'fire water', perhaps we'd now call it Frisky. We digress.

'Whisky' or 'whiskey' is a common spelling conundrum but the correct name is simply determined by where it was made. As a general rule, 'whisky' is made in Scotland, Canada and the rest of the world, while Ireland and America use 'whiskey'. And where whisk(e)y comes from is of great importance to a lot of people in a lot of places.

From America's smooth, corn mash bourbons and rye-y ryes, to Ireland's triple-distilled blends and Scotland's famed single malts (and every combination and exception in between), Whisky is a whole w(h)ide w(h)orld of w(h)ater - life and/or fire - to discover.

In this collection you'll find recipes that'll help you do just that.

# RUM

RUM is a distilled spirit made from sugarcane and is usually aged in barrels.

Hailing from the Caribbean, it was first distilled on sugarcane plantations back in the 17th century and found its way across the seven seas under all sorts of psuedonyms that give us a pretty good idea of its original tasting notes.

This Nelson's blood, or kill-devil demon water, was imbibed to combat scurvy, warm the cockles and put the 'irate in pirate. Thankfully, some clever coves recognised it as having the potential to be a jolly good snifter and refined it a little.

Rum now comes in various grades across a honeyed-in-colour and sugar-and-spice-in-flavour spectrum. From light, almost clear, to golden, dark and stormy, it is all caramel, banana, chocolate, ginger, vanilla and cinnamon. Pirates' grog it ain't.

This book contains an array of cocktail recipes with rum at their ar-me-hearty heart. From the sweet-sour, lip-smacking Daiquiri, and the hello sunshine, make mine a Piña Colada, to the garden party favourite Long Island Iced Tea, it's 'Yo-ho-ho and a bottle of rum' and, no, not a bottle. Please, drink responsibly.

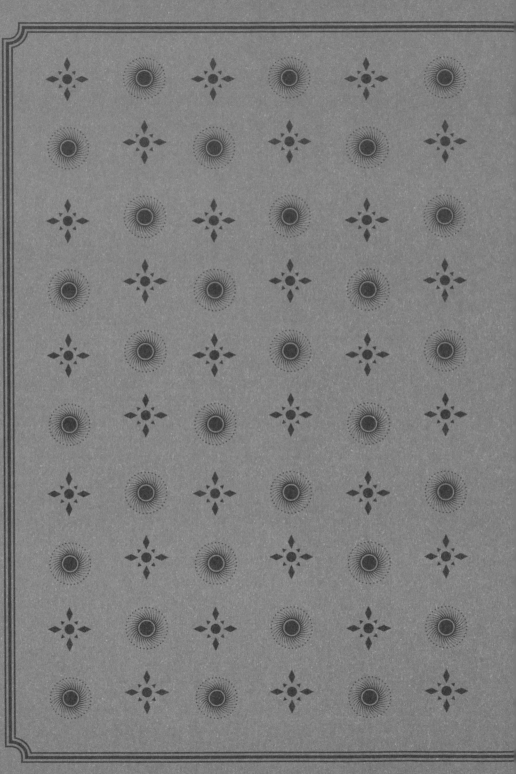

# LIGHT & FLORAL

# GIN CUCUMBER COOLER

**2 MEASURES GIN**

**5 MINT LEAVES**

**5 SLICES CUCUMBER**

**3 MEASURES APPLE JUICE**

**3 MEASURES SODA WATER**

**MINT, TO GARNISH**

Add the gin, mint and cucumber to a glass and gently muddle.

Leave to stand for a couple of minutes, then add the apple juice, soda water and some ice cubes.

Garnish with a sprig of mint.

# FRENCH AFTERNOON

1 MEASURE GIN

3 TSP CAMOMILE TEA SYRUP

3 TSP LEMON JUICE

2 DASHES PEACH BITTERS

CHAMPAGNE, TO TOP

LEMON, TO GARNISH

Add all the ingredients except the Champagne to a cocktail shaker and shake and strain into a flute glass.

Top up with 4 measures chilled Champagne and garnish with a lemon twist.

# GIN GARDEN MARTINI

**4 MEASURES GIN**

**1 MEASURE ELDERFLOWER CORDIAL**

**½ CUCUMBER, PEELED AND CHOPPED**

**2 MEASURES PRESSED APPLE JUICE**

**CUCUMBER, TO GARNISH**

Muddle the cucumber in the bottom of a cocktail shaker with the elderflower cordial.

Add the gin, apple juice and some ice cubes and shake and double-strain into 2 chilled martini glasses.

Garnish with peeled cucumber slices.

# CAMOMILE COLLINS

2 MEASURES GIN

1 CAMOMILE TEA BAG

1 MEASURE LEMON JUICE

1 MEASURE SUGAR SYRUP

4 MEASURES SODA WATER

LEMON, TO GARNISH

Pour the gin into a glass and add the tea bag.

Stir the tea bag and gin together, for about 5 minutes, until the gin is infused with camomile flavour.

Remove the tea bag and fill the glass with ice cubes.

Add the remaining ingredients and garnish with a lemon slice.

# STRAWBERRY FIELDS

2 MEASURES GIN

1 CAMOMILE TEA BAG

1 MEASURE STRAWBERRY PURÉE

2 TSP LEMON JUICE

1 MEASURE DOUBLE CREAM

3 TSP EGG WHITE

SODA WATER, TO TOP

STRAWBERRY, TO GARNISH

Place 1 camomile tea bag and 2 measures gin in a cocktail shaker and leave to infuse for 2 minutes.

Remove the tea bag and add the rest of the ingredients to the shaker.

Shake and strain into a wine glass and top up with 4 measures chilled soda water.

Garnish with a strawberry.

# HONG KONG SLING

½ MEASURE GIN

½ MEASURE LYCHEE LIQUEUR

1 MEASURE LYCHEE PURÉE

1 MEASURE LEMON JUICE

½ MEASURE SUGAR SYRUP

SODA WATER, TO TOP

FRESH LYCHEE IN ITS SHELL, TO GARNISH

Add all the ingredients except the soda water to a cocktail shaker and shake and strain into a sling glass.

Top up with soda water, garnish with a lychee and serve with long straws.

# LEMON GRASS COLLINS

**4 MEASURES LEMON GRASS-INFUSED**

**VODKA (SEE PAGE 209)**

**½ MEASURE VANILLA LIQUEUR**

**DASH LEMON JUICE**

**DASH SUGAR SYRUP**

**GINGER BEER, TO TOP**

Divide 4 measures lemon grass-infused vodka between 2 highball glasses full of crushed ice.

Then add ½ measure vanilla liqueur and 1 dash lemon juice to each.

Add sugar syrup to taste and top up with ginger beer.

# CAMOMILE SANGRIA

1 MEASURE VODKA

2 MEASURES WHITE WINE

1 CAMOMILE TEA BAG

2 TSP PASSION FRUIT SYRUP

1 TSP LEMON JUICE

5 WHITE GRAPES

2 MEASURES SODA WATER

APPLE, TO GARNISH

Add 1 camomile tea bag and 1 measure vodka to a cocktail shaker and leave to infuse for 3 minutes.

Remove the tea bag, add 5 white grapes and muddle, then add the remaining ingredients.

Shake and strain into a sling glass full of ice cubes, top up with 2 measures soda water, and garnish with an apple wedge.

# BELLINI-TINI

**2 MEASURES VODKA**

**½ MEASURE PEACH SCHNAPPS**

**2 TSP PEACH JUICE**

**CHAMPAGNE, TO TOP**

**PEACH SLICES, TO GARNISH**

Put the vodka, schnapps and peach juice into a cocktail shaker and shake well.

Pour into a cocktail glass and top up with Champagne.

Garnish with peach slices.

# PEPPERMINT RICKY

**1 MEASURE VODKA**

**1 PEPPERMINT TEA BAG**

**3 LIME WEDGES, PLUS EXTRA, TO GARNISH**

**5 MEASURES SODA WATER**

Put 1 measure vodka and 1 peppermint tea bag in a collins glass and leave to infuse for 3 minutes.

Remove the tea bag and add ice cubes to fill the glass.

Add 3 lime wedges and 4 measures soda water and stir.

Garnish with an extra wedge of lime.

33

# NEW DAWN COOLER

**1 MEASURE VODKA**

**2 MEASURES APPLE JUICE**

**½ MEASURE PASSION FRUIT SYRUP**

**PROSECCO, TO TOP**

**GRAPES, TO GARNISH**

Add all the ingredients except the Prosecco to a highball glass filled with cubed ice.

Stir well, top with chilled Prosecco and garnish with white grapes.

# ORCHARD BELLINI

½ RIPE WHITE PEACH

1 MEASURE APPLE JUICE

DASH OF SUGAR SYRUP

PROSECCO, TO TOP

Add the peach and sugar syrup to a blender or food processor and blend until smooth.

Pour into a Champagne flute with the apple juice and the sugar syrup and top with chilled Prosecco.

36

# LYCHEE & APEROL

**2 MEASURES APEROL**

**2 MEASURES LYCHEE JUICE**

**PROSECCO, TO TOP**

**ORANGE, TO GARNISH**

Add the Aperol and lychee juice to a wine glass filled with cubed ice.

Stir well, top with chilled Prosecco and garnish with a slice of orange.

# PRIMROSE FIZZ

**½ MEASURE ELDERFLOWER CORDIAL**

**1 MEASURE APPLE JUICE**

**6 MINT LEAVES**

**PROSECCO, TO TOP**

**APPLE, TO GARNISH**

Squeeze the mint leaves in your hand to express the oils, then drop them into a wine glass.

Add the elderflower cordial and apple juice, fill with cubed ice and top with chilled Prosecco.

Stir briefly and garnish with apple slices.

# FLORAL BELLINI

½ MEASURE ROSE LIQUEUR

1 TSP LAVENDER SYRUP

2 MEASURES GRAPEFRUIT JUICE

PROSECCO, TO TOP

DRIED LAVENDER FLOWERS, TO GARNISH

Pour the rose liqueur, lavender syrup and grapefruit juice into a cocktail shaker or mixing glass filled with cubed ice.

Stir for 10 seconds and strain into a Champagne flute.

Top with chilled Prosecco and garnish with dried lavender flowers.

# COTTER KIR

**2 TSP CRÈME DE CASSIS**

**2 TSP RASPBERRY LIQUEUR**

**1 MEASURE CRANBERRY JUICE**

**PROSECCO, TO TOP**

**RASPBERRIES, TO GARNISH**

Add all the ingredients except
the Prosecco to a wine glass filled
with cubed ice and stir briefly.

Top with chilled Prosecco and
garnish with raspberries.

*41*

# STONE FENCE

**1 CRISP APPLE, PLUS AN APPLE SLICE, TO GARNISH**

**2 MEASURES RYE WHISKEY**

**1 MEASURE SODA WATER**

Juice the apple and pour into a glass full of ice cubes.

Add the whiskey and soda water and garnish with an apple slice.

# ICHI HIGHBALL

**1½ MEASURES SCOTCH WHISKY**

**1 MEASURE UMESHU**

**SODA WATER, TO TOP**

**4 CUCUMBER SLICES, PLUS EXTRA STRIPS,**

**TO GARNISH**

Add 4 cucumber slices, 1 measure umeshu and 1½ measures Scotch whisky to a glass and press the cucumber with the end of a bar spoon to release some of the flavour.

Fill a collins glass with ice cubes, top with 4 measures soda water and stir.

Garnish with a cucumber strip.

# MINT JULEP II

**1 MEASURE BOURBON**

**½ TBSP CASTER SUGAR**

**1 TBSP SODA WATER**

**3 SPRIGS MINT, PLUS EXTRA, TO GARNISH**

Crush the mint with the sugar in an old-fashioned glass or large tumbler and rub it around the insides of the glass. Discard the mint.

Dissolve the sugar in the soda water, add 3–4 ice cubes and pour the bourbon over it. Do not stir.

Garnish with the extra mint sprig.

# ITALIAN HEATHER

**4 MEASURES SCOTCH WHISKY**

**1 MEASURE GALLIANO**

**LEMON, TO GARNISH**

Put the ice cubes into a tall glass and stir in the whisky and Galliano.

Garnish with a lemon rind twist.

# VIRGINIA MINT JULEP

**3 MEASURES BOURBON**

**1 TSP SUGAR SYRUP**

**9 YOUNG MINT SPRIGS, PLUS EXTRA, TO GARNISH**

Muddle the mint and sugar syrup in an iced silver mug or tall glass.

Fill the mug or glass with crushed ice, pour the bourbon over the ice and stir gently.

Pack in more crushed ice and stir until a frost forms.

Wrap the mug or glass in a table napkin and garnish with a mint sprig.

# PINEAPPLE MOJITO

2 MEASURES GOLDEN RUM

½ LIME, HALVED

6 MINT LEAVES

4 PINEAPPLE CHUNKS

2 TSP SOFT BROWN SUGAR

PINEAPPLE JUICE, TO TOP

PINEAPPLE & MINT SPRIG, TO GARNISH

Muddle the mint leaves, pineapple chunks, lime and sugar in a cocktail shaker. Add the rum and shake well.

Strain into a highball glass filled with crushed ice, top up with pineapple juice and stir.

Garnish with a pineapple wedge and a mint sprig and serve with straws.

# APPLE-SOAKED MOJITO

**2 MEASURES GOLDEN RUM**

**8 MINT LEAVES, PLUS AN EXTRA SPRIG, TO GARNISH**

**½ LIME, CUT INTO WEDGES**

**2 TSP SUGAR SYRUP**

**2 MEASURES GOLDEN RUM**

**APPLE JUICE, TO TOP**

**MINT SPRIG & RED APPLE, TO GARNISH**

Muddle the mint leaves, lime wedges and sugar syrup in a cocktail shaker.

Add the rum, shake well and strain into a highball glass filled with crushed ice.

Top with apple juice and garnish with a mint sprig and an apple slice.

# COOPER COOLER

**2 MEASURES GOLDEN RUM**

**3 MEASURES DRY GINGER ALE**

**1 TBSP LIME OR LEMON JUICE**

**LIME OR LEMON, TO GARNISH**

Put some ice cubes into a highball glass.

Pour over the rum, ginger ale and lime or lemon juice and stir.

Garnish with a lime or lemon slice.

*51*

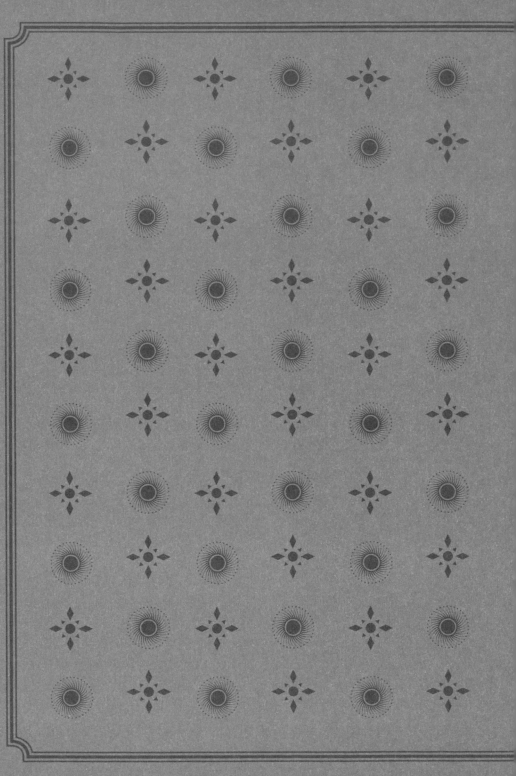

# VIBRANT & ZESTY

# MARTINEZ

**2 MEASURES GIN**

**3 TSP SWEET VERMOUTH**

**2 TSP ORANGE LIQUEUR**

**2 DASHES ANGOSTURA BITTERS**

**ORANGE, TO GARNISH**

Fill a glass with ice and add the remaining ingredients.

Stir and garnish with an orange twist.

# THE FIX

**4 MEASURES GIN**

**1 MEASURE COINTREAU**

**1 DASH LIME JUICE**

**1 DASH LEMON JUICE**

**1 DASH PINEAPPLE JUICE**

Add all the ingredients to a cocktail shaker filled with ice.

Shake and strain into 2 chilled highball glasses.

# HONEYDEW

**1 MEASURE GIN**

**½ MEASURE LEMON JUICE**

**½ MEASURE SUGAR SYRUP**

**2 DROPS ABSINTHE (OR PERNOD)**

**5 CUBES HONEYDEW MELON**

**PROSECCO, TO TOP**

**LEMON & ROSEMARY, TO GARNISH**

Add all the ingredients except the Prosecco to a blender or food processor and blend with 5 cubes of ice.

Pour into a chilled wine glass, top with chilled Prosecco and garnish with a lemon twist and a sprig of rosemary.

57

# SOUTHSIDE

**2 MEASURES GIN**

**4 TSP LIME JUICE**

**4 TSP SUGAR SYRUP**

**5 MINT LEAVES**

**MINT, TO GARNISH**

Add all the ingredients to a cocktail shaker and shake and strain into a cocktail glass.

Garnish with a mint leaf.

# KIWI SMASH

**2 MEASURES GIN**

**½ KIWI FRUIT, QUARTERED**

**4 SLICES LEMON**

**4 TSP SUGAR SYRUP**

**1 SPRIG CORIANDER**

**KIWI FRUIT, TO GARNISH**

Add the kiwi fruit, lemon and sugar syrup to a glass and muddle.

Add the gin and coriander and half-fill the glass with crushed ice.

Churn with the muddler until thoroughly mixed and top up with more crushed ice.

Garnish with a kiwi fruit slice.

# BETSY

**2 MEASURES GIN OR VODKA**

**4 TSP LIME JUICE**

**1 MEASURE SUGAR SYRUP**

**2 STRAWBERRIES**

**1 SPRIG CORIANDER**

**STRAWBERRIES, TO GARNISH**

Add all the ingredients, plus a cup of ice cubes, to a food processor or blender and blend until smooth.

Pour into 2 glasses and garnish each with a strawberry.

# VALENTINE MARTINI

**4 MEASURES RASPBERRY VODKA**

**12 RASPBERRIES, PLUS EXTRA, TO GARNISH**

**1 MEASURE LIME JUICE**

**2 DASHES SUGAR SYRUP**

**LIME, TO GARNISH**

Half-fill a cocktail shaker with ice cubes. Add all the remaining ingredients and shake until a frost forms on the outside of the shaker.

Double-strain into 2 chilled martini glasses.

Garnish with raspberries and lime rind spirals on cocktail sticks.

# LONG BLUSH

1 MEASURE VODKA

2 TSP HONEY

1 MEASURE POMEGRANATE JUICE

2 TSP LIME JUICE

1 MEASURE ROSÉ WINE

5 MINT LEAVES

2 MEASURES SODA WATER

MINT SPRIG & POMEGRANATE SEEDS,

TO GARNISH

Add add the ingredients except the soda water to a cocktail shaker and shake and strain into glass.

Add the soda water, top up the glass with crushed ice and garnish with a mint sprig and some pomegranate seeds.

# SEA BREEZE

**2 MEASURES VODKA**

**4 MEASURES CRANBERRY JUICE**

**2 MEASURES GRAPEFRUIT JUICE**

**LIME, TO GARNISH**

Fill 2 highball glasses with ice cubes, pour over the vodka, cranberry juice and grapefruit juice and stir well.

Garnish with lime wedges.

# BLANC MONT BLANC

1 MEASURE VODKA

1 MEASURE BLANC VERMOUTH

5 WHITE GRAPES, PLUS EXTRA, TO GARNISH

1 MEASURE LEMON JUICE

1 MEASURE SUGAR SYRUP

Muddle the grapes at the base of a cocktail shaker.

Add the vodka, blanc vermouth, lemon juice and sugar syrup.

Fill the shaker with ice cubes, shake and strain into a martini glass.

Garnish with grapes.

# RISING SUN

**4 MEASURES VODKA**

**4 TSP PASSION FRUIT SYRUP**

**6 MEASURES GRAPEFRUIT JUICE**

**PINK GRAPEFRUIT, TO GARNISH**

Half-fill a cocktail shaker with ice cubes and put 6–8 ice cubes into each old-fashioned glass.

Add all the remaining ingredients to the shaker and shake until a frost forms on the outside of the shaker.

Strain over the ice in the glasses and garnish each with a pink grapefruit slice.

# LOS ALTOS

2 MEASURES TEQUILA

½ MEASURE LIME JUICE

2 MEASURES ORANGE JUICE

3 TSP AGAVE SYRUP

2 TSP CAMPARI

PROSECCO, TO TOP

ORANGE & LIME, TO GARNISH

Add all the ingredients except the Prosecco to your cocktail shaker, shake and strain into a hurricane glass filled with cubed ice.

Top with chilled Prosecco and garnish with a lime wedge and a slice of orange.

# TANKA COBBLER

**1 MEASURE FINO SHERRY**

**½ MEASURE LEMON JUICE**

**2 TSP SUGAR SYRUP**

**4 RASPBERRIES**

**PROSECCO, TO TOP**

**RASPBERRIES, TO GARNISH**

Add the Fino Sherry, lemon juice, sugar syrup and raspberries to your cocktail shaker.

Shake well and strain into to highball glass filled with crushed ice.

Top with chilled Prosecco and more crushed ice and garnish with raspberries.

71

# GOLDEN APRICOT

**1 MEASURE RUM**

**½ MEASURE APRICOT LIQUEUR**

**½ MEASURE LIME JUICE**

**2 TSP SUGAR SYRUP**

**PROSECCO, TO TOP**

**LIME, TO GARNISH**

Add all ingredients to a highball glass filled with cubed ice and stir well.

Top with chilled Prosecco and garnish with a lime wedge.

# PASSION FRUIT SPRITZ

1 MEASURE VANILLA VODKA

1 MEASURE PASSION FRUIT SYRUP

½ MEASURE LEMON JUICE

PROSECCO, TO TOP

MINT & PASSIONFRUIT, TO GARNISH

Add the vodka, passion fruit syrup and lemon juice to a wine glass filled with cubed ice.

Stir well, top with chilled Prosecco and garnish with half a passion fruit and a sprig of mint.

# PEACHES & GREEN

1 MEASURE VODKA

1 MEASURE GREEN TEA, CHILLED

½ RIPE WHITE PEACH

1 TSP LEMON JUICE

1 DASH SUGAR SYRUP

PROSECCO, TO TOP

Add all the ingredients except the Prosecco to a blender or food processor and blend until smooth.

Pour into a wine glass filled with cubed ice and top with chilled Prosecco.

# MANDARIN 75

1 MEASURE COINTREAU

½ MEASURE LEMON JUICE

2 TSP SUGAR SYRUP

PROSECCO, TO TOP

ORANGE, TO GARNISH

Add the Cointreau, lemon juice and sugar syrup to a chilled Champagne flute.

Top with chilled Prosecco and garnish with an orange twist.

# CHUCK BUCK MULE

**2 MEASURES ORANGE & CHERRY-INFUSED**

**BOURBON (SEE PAGE 209)**

**4 TSP TRIPLE SEC**

**2 TSP LEMON JUICE**

**2 TSP GINGER JUICE**

**MARASCHINO CHERRY OR ORANGE, TO GARNISH**

Fill a collins glass with ice cubes, add all the ingredients except the soda water and stir.

Top up with 4 measures soda water and garnish with a maraschino cherry or orange slice.

# GOLDEN DAISY

**3 MEASURES SCOTCH WHISKY**

**½ MEASURE COINTREAU**

**JUICE OF 1 LEMON**

**1 TSP SUGAR SYRUP**

**LIME, TO GARNISH**

Put 4–5 ice cubes into a cocktail shaker and pour the whisky, Cointreau, lemon juice and sugar syrup over it.

Shake until a frost forms and strain into an old-fashioned glass.

Garnish with a lime wedge.

79

# PEACH SMASH

**4 MEASURES BOURBON**

**12 MINT LEAVES, PLUS SPRIGS, TO GARNISH**

**6 PEACH SLICES**

**4 TSP CASTER SUGAR**

**6 LEMON SLICES, PLUS EXTRA, TO GARNISH**

Muddle the mint leaves, peach and lemon slices and sugar in a cocktail shaker.

Add the bourbon and some ice cubes and shake well.

Strain over cracked ice into 2 glasses and garnish each with a mint sprig and a lemon slice.

# WILLIAM'S PEAR

**2 MEASURES BOURBON**

**4 TSP LEMON JUICE**

**½ RIPE PEAR CUT INTO CHUNKS,**

**PLUS EXTRA SLICES, TO GARNISH**

**3 TSP REDCURRANT JAM**

**2 TSP SUGAR SYRUP**

Add the pear and jam to a cocktail shaker and muddle.

Add the remaining ingredients and shake and strain into a glass full of ice cubes

Garnish with pear slices.

# SPICED PEAR COCKTAIL

**1½ MEASURES BOURBON**

**2 TSP BÉNÉDICTINE**

**2 TSP NUTMEG SYRUP**

**2 TSP LEMON JUICE**

**10 REDCURRANTS**

**½ RIPE PEAR, PLUS EXTRA, TO GARNISH**

Add ½ ripe pear, cut into chunks, and 10 redcurrants to a cocktail shaker and muddle.

Add the remaining ingredients and shake.

Strain into an old-fashioned glass full of ice cubes and garnish with pear slices.

# SCOTCH GINGER HIGHBALL

**2 MEASURES SCOTCH WHISKY**

**1 MEASURE LEMON JUICE**

**3 TSP SUGAR SYRUP**

**4 MEASURES GINGER ALE**

**FRESH ROOT GINGER, TO GARNISH**

Pour the whisky, lemon juice, sugar syrup and ginger ale into a glass filled with ice cubes and stir.

Garnish with a slice of fresh root ginger.

# STRAWBERRY DAIQUIRI

**2 MEASURES GOLDEN RUM**

**2 MEASURES LIME JUICE**

**3 STRAWBERRIES, HULLED**

**DASH OF STRAWBERRY SYRUP**

**6 MINT LEAVES, PLUS A SPRIG TO GARNISH**

**STRAWBERRY, TO GARNISH**

Muddle the strawberries, syrup and mint leaves in the bottom of a cocktail shaker.

Add the rum and lime juice, shake with ice and double-strain into a chilled martini glass.

Garnish with a strawberry slice and a sprig of mint.

# BAIJAN SWIZZLE

**1 MEASURE WHITE RUM**

**3 TSP FALERNUM**

**4 TSP LIME JUICE**

**2 DASHES ANGOSTURA BITTERS**

**5 MINT LEAVES**

**MINT SPRING, TO GARNISH**

Add all the ingredients to a sling glass half filled with crushed ice and swizzle the drink by spinning a bar spoon between the two flat palms of your hand.

Top the glass up with crushed ice, garnish with a mint sprig.

# LIMON MOJITO

**4 MEASURES LEMON BACARDI**

**2 LIMES, QUARTERED**

**4 TSP SOFT BROWN SUGAR**

**16 MINT LEAVES**

**SODA WATER, TO TOP**

**LEMON & LIME, TO GARNISH**

Muddle the quarters of 2 limes with 4 teaspoons soft brown sugar and 16 mint leaves in the bottom of 2 highball glasses, then add 4 measures Limon Bacardi.

Stir and top up with soda water.

Garnish with lemon and lime slices and serve with straws.

# RUM COLLINS

**2 MEASURES WHITE RUM**

**1 TSP CASTER SUGAR**

**1 DASH ORANGE BITTERS**

**2 TSP LEMON JUICE**

**3 MEASURES SODA WATER**

**LEMON & ORANGE, TO GARNISH**

Add the rum and sugar to a glass and stir until the sugar has dissolved. Then add the orange bitters and lemon juice.

Fill the glass with ice cubes, top up with the soda water, then stir.

Garnish with a lemon and orange wedge.

*91*

# MELON DAIQUIRI

**2 MEASURES RUM**

**1 MEASURE LIME JUICE**

**½ MEASURE MIDORI**

**MELON, TO GARNISH**

Add all the ingredients, plus some
some crushed ice, to a cocktail
shaker.

Shake and strain into a chilled
martini glass and garnish with a
small wedge of melon.

# COCONUT DAIQUIRI

**2 MEASURES WHITE RUM**

**1 MEASURE COCONUT LIQUEUR**

**2 MEASURES LIME JUICE**

**1 TSP GRENADINE**

**LIME, TO GARNISH**

Put 4–5 crushed ice cubes into a cocktail shaker and pour over the remaining ingredients.

Shake until a frost forms and strain into a cocktail glass and garnish with a lime slice.

*93*

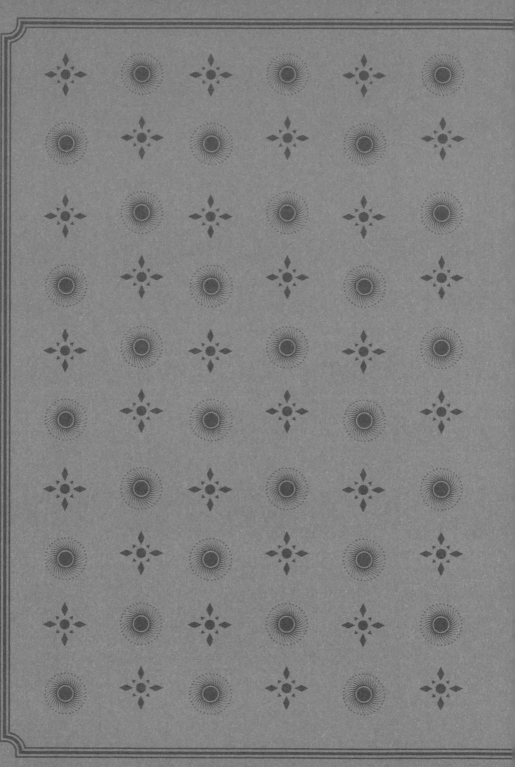

# INTENSE
# & SULTRY

# MOON RIVER

1 MEASURE DRY GIN

1 MEASURE APRICOT BRANDY

1 MEASURE COINTREAU

½ MEASURE GALLIANO

½ MEASURE LEMON JUICE

MARASCHINO CHERRIES, TO GARNISH

Put some ice cubes into a cocktail shaker and add the rest of the ingredients.

Shake, then strain, into 2 large chilled martini glasses.

Garnish each with a cherry.

96

# SINGAPORE SLING

**2 MEASURES GIN**

**1 MEASURE CHERRY BRANDY**

**½ MEASURE COINTREAU**

**½ MEASURE BÉNÉDICTINE**

**1 MEASURE GRENADINE**

**1 MEASURE LIME JUICE**

**10 MEASURES PINEAPPLE JUICE**

**1–2 DASHES ANGOSTURA BITTERS**

**PINEAPPLE & MARASCHINO CHERRIES,**

**TO GARNISH**

Half-fill a cocktail shaker with ice cubes, add the remaining ingredients and shake until a frost forms on the outside of the shaker.

Strain into 2 highball glasses and garnish each one with a pineapple wedge and a maraschino cherry.

# ZED

1 MEASURE GIN

1 MEASURE MANDARINE NAPOLÉON BRANDY

3 MEASURES PINEAPPLE JUICE

1 TSP SUGAR

LEMON, MINT, PINEAPPLE & ORANGE,

TO GARNISH

Put cracked ice into a cocktail shaker and pour the gin, Mandarine Napoléon, pineapple juice and sugar over it.

Shake lightly to mix and pour into a tall glass.

Garnish with half lemon slices, a mint sprig, a pineapple wedge and orange rind strips.

# BERRY COLLINS

**8 BLUEBERRIES**

**1–2 DASHES STRAWBERRY SYRUP**

**4 MEASURES GIN**

**4 TSP LEMON JUICE**

**SUGAR SYRUP, TO TASTE**

**SODA WATER, TO TOP**

**LEMON, RASPBERRIES & BLUEBERRIES,**

**TO GARNISH**

Muddle the berries and strawberry syrup in the bottom of each glass, then fill each glass with crushed ice.

Add the gin, lemon juice and sugar syrup.

Stir, then top up with the soda water.

Garnish with the berries and a lemon slice.

# GIN SLING

**6 MEASURES GIN**

**2 MEASURES CHERRY BRANDY**

**JUICE OF 1 LEMON**

**SODA WATER, TO TOP**

Add all the ingredients except the soda water to a cocktail shaker and shake with plenty of ice.

Strain into 2 highball glasses filled with ice and top up with soda water.

# BITTERSWEET SYMPHONY

**1 MEASURE GIN**

**1 MEASURE CAMPARI**

**½ MEASURE PASSION FRUIT SYRUP**

**½ MEASURE LEMON JUICE**

**LEMON, TO GARNISH**

Put some ice cubes into a cocktail shaker with all the ingredients and shake to mix.

Strain into an old-fashioned glass over 4–6 ice cubes and garnish with lemon slices.

# GODMOTHER

**3 MEASURES VODKA**

**1 MEASURE AMARETTO DI SARONNO**

Put 4–6 cracked ice cubes
into 2 old-fashioned glasses.

Add the vodka and Amaretto,
stir lightly to mix and serve.

# DUTCH ROSE

**1 ½ MEASURS VODKA**

**2 TSP ORANGE LIQUEUR**

**2 TSP DRY VERMOUTH**

**2 DASHES ORANGE BITTERS**

**DASH ORANGE BLOSSOM WATER**

**1 TSP GRENADINE**

**ORANGE, TO GARNISH**

Add all the ingredients to a martini glass filled with ice cubes and stir.

Garnish with an orange twist.

# ST PETERSBURG

**3 MEASURES VODKA**

**1 MEASURE CHARTREUSE**

Put 4–6 cracked ice cubes into
2 old-fashioned glasses.

Add the vodka and Chartreuse,
stir lightly to mix and serve.

# MUDSLIDE

**1 MEASURE VODKA**

**1 MEASURE KAHLÚA**

**1 MEASURE BAILEYS IRISH CREAM**

Put 6 cracked ice cubes into a cocktail shaker and add the vodka, Kahlúa and Baileys.

Shake until a frost forms.

Strain into a tumbler and add the some more cracked ice.

# TOKYO JOE

**1 MEASURE VODKA**

**1 MEASURE MIDORI**

Put some ice cubes into a cocktail shaker, add the vodka and Midori and shake well.

Strain into an old-fashioned glass, over ice cubes if you like.

# CELEBRATION COCKTAIL

**1 MEASURE COGNAC**

**1 TSP CRÈME DE MURE**

**1 TSP BENEDICTINE**

**1  LEMON WEDGE**

**CASTER SUGAR**

**PROSECCO, TO TOP**

Frost the rim of a Champagne flute by moistening it with the lemon wedge and dipping it in the caster sugar.

Add the Cognac, Crème de Mure and Benedictine to the glass and top with chilled Prosecco.

# G & TEA SPRITZ

½ MEASURE STRAWBERRY LIQUEUR

1 TSP LEMON JUICE

1 TSP SUGAR SYRUP

2 MEASURES EARL GREY TEA, CHILLED

PROSECCO, TO TOP

MINT, TO GARNISH

Add all the ingredients except the Prosecco to a wine glass filled with cubed ice.

Top with chilled Prosecco and garnish with a mint sprig.

# RUBY TUESDAY

**1 MEASURE RUM**

**½ MEASURE LIME JUICE**

**½ MEASURE SUGAR SYRUP**

**6 RASPBERRIES**

**PROSECCO, TO TOP**

**RASPBERRY, TO GARNISH**

Add the rum, lime juice, sugar syrup and raspberries to a blender or food processor and blend until smooth.

Pour into a Champagne flute and top with chilled Prosecco.

Garnish with a raspberry.

# PINK SANGRIA

**2 MEASURES ROSÉ WINE**

**1 ½ MEASURES POMEGRANATE JUICE**

**2 TSP AGAVE SYRUP**

**PROSECCO, TO TOP**

**PINK GRAPEFRUIT, TO GARNISH**

Add all ingredients except the Prosecco to a wine glass filled with cubed ice.

Stir briefly, top with chilled Prosecco and garnish with a slice of pink grapefruit.

# BUBBLE BERRY

½ MEASURE RASPBERRY LIQUEUR

½ MEASURE BLACKBERRY LIQUEUR

PROSECCO, TO TOP

RASPBERRY & BLACKBERRY, TO GARNISH

Add the liqueurs to a Champagne flute and top with chilled Prosecco.

Drop in a raspberry and a blackberry to garnish.

# DEVIL'S ADVOCATE

½ MEASURE CAMPARI

1 MEASURE BLOOD ORANGE JUICE

½ MEASURE SUGAR SYRUP

PROSECCO, TO TOP

ORANGE, TO GARNISH

Add the cognac, Cointreau and sugar syrup into a cocktail shaker or mixing glass filled with cubed ice.

Stir for 10 seconds and strain into a Champagne flute.

Top with chilled Prosecco and garnish with a twist of orange.

# GINGER FIX

**1 MEASURE BLENDED SCOTCH WHISKY**

**1 MEASURE GINGER WINE**

**2 DASHES ANGOSTURA BITTERS**

**4 MEASURES SODA WATER**

**LEMON, TO GARNISH**

Fill the glass with ice cubes, add the remaining ingredients and stir.

Garnish with a lemon wedge.

# RITZ
# OLD FASHIONED

1½ MEASURES BOURBON

½ MEASURE GRAND MARNIER

1 DASH LEMON JUICE, PLUS EXTRA,

TO FROST THE GLASS

1 DASH ANGOSTURA BITTERS

CASTER SUGAR

ORANGE OR LEMON, TO GARNISH

Frost the rim of a cocktail glass by dipping it into lemon juice, then pressing it into the sugar.

Put a few crushed ice cubes into a cocktail shaker and add the remaining ingredients.

Shake to mix, strain into the prepared glass and garnish with an orange or lemon rind spiral.

# BLACK JACK

¾ MEASURE JACK DANIEL'S

¾ MEASURE BLACK SAMBUCA

Pour the Jack Daniel's into a
shot glass.

Using the back of a bar spoon,
slowly float the sambuca over
the Jack Daniel's.

# WHISKY HIGHBALL

**2 MEASURES SCOTCH WHISKY**

**1 DASH ANGOSTURA BITTERS**

**4 MEASURES SODA WATER**

**LEMON, TO GARNISH**

Add 3 large ice cubes, the whisky and Angostura bitters to a glass.

Stir gently, then fill the glass with more ice cubes and top up with the soda water.

Garnish with a lemon twist.

# ZOOM

**2 MEASURES SCOTCH WHISKY**

**1 TSP CLEAR HONEY**

**1 MEASURE CHILLED WATER**

**1 MEASURE SINGLE CREAM**

Put some ice cubes into a cocktail shaker, add the whisky, honey, chilled water and cream and shake well.

Strain into an old-fashioned glass.

# BOBBY BURNS

**1 MEASURE SCOTCH WHISKY**

**1 MEASURE DRY VERMOUTH**

**1 TBSP BÉNÉDICTINE**

**LEMON, TO GARNISH**

Put some ice cubes into a cocktail shaker with the whisky, vermouth and Bénédictine and shake until a frost forms.

Strain into a chilled cocktail glass and garnish with a lemon rind strip.

# RUM OLD FASHIONED

**2 MEASURES WHITE RUM**

**½ MEASURE DARK RUM**

**1 DASH ANGOSTURA BITTERS**

**1 DASH LIME BITTERS**

**1 TSP CASTER SUGAR**

**½ MEASURE WATER**

**CHERRY, TO GARNISH**

Stir 1 ice cube with the bitters, sugar and water in a heavy-based old-fashioned glass until the sugar has dissolved.

Add the white rum, stir and add the some more ice cubes.

Add the dark rum and stir once again.

Garnish with a cherry.

# ST LUCIA

**2 MEASURES WHITE OR GOLDEN RUM**

**1 MEASURE CURAÇAO**

**1 MEASURE DRY VERMOUTH**

**1 TSP GRENADINE**

**JUICE OF ½ ORANGE**

**ORANGE & COCKTAIL CHERRY, TO GARNISH**

Put 4–5 ice cubes into a cocktail shaker and pour over the Curaçao, vermouth, orange juice, grenadine and rum.

Shake until a frost forms, then pour without straining into a highball glass.

Garnish with an orange rind spiral and a cocktail cherry.

# RUM CRUSTA

2 MEASURES DARK RUM

1 MEASURE COINTREAU

2 TSP MARASCHINO LIQUEUR

2 TSP LIME JUICE

LIME WEDGE

CASTER SUGAR

2 GRAPES, TO GARNISH

Frost the rim of an old-fashioned glass by moistening it with the lime wedge and pressing it into the sugar.

Put some ice cubes into a cocktail shaker with the rum, Cointreau, Maraschino liqueur and lime juice and shake well.

Strain into an old-fashioned glass filled with crushed ice and garnish with the grapes.

# HAVANA ZOMBIE

1 MEASURE WHITE RUM

1 MEASURE GOLDEN RUM

1 MEASURE DARK RUM

JUICE OF 1 LIME

5 TBSP PINEAPPLE JUICE

1 TSP SUGAR SYRUP

Put 4–5 ice cubes into a mixing glass.

Pour the fruit juices, sugar syrup and rums over the ice and stir vigorously.

Pour without straining into a tall glass.

# CAPRISSIMA DA FRAMOESA

2 MEASURES AMBER RUM

2 TSP RASPBERRY LIQUEUR

1 TSP PASTIS

½ LIME

5 RASPBERRIES

2 PINK GRAPEFRUIT SLICES

3 TSP SUGAR SYRUP

PINK GRAPEFRUIT & RASPBERRY, TO GARNISH

Muddle ½ lime, 5 raspberries and 1 teaspoon pastis in a collins glass.

Add the remaining ingredients and half-fill the glass with crushed ice. Churn with a muddler until thoroughly mixed.

Top up the glass with more crushed ice, garnish with a raspberry and a pink grapefruit wedge.

# HUMMINGBIRD

**1 MEASURE DARK RUM**

**1 MEASURE LIGHT RUM**

**1 MEASURE SOUTHERN COMFORT**

**1 MEASURE ORANGE JUICE**

**COLA, TO TOP**

**ORANGE, TO GARNISH**

Put some crushed ice into a cocktail shaker and pour the rums, Southern Comfort and orange juice over it.

Shake until a frost forms, strain into a long glass and top up with cola.

Garnish with an orange slice and serve with a straw.

*133*

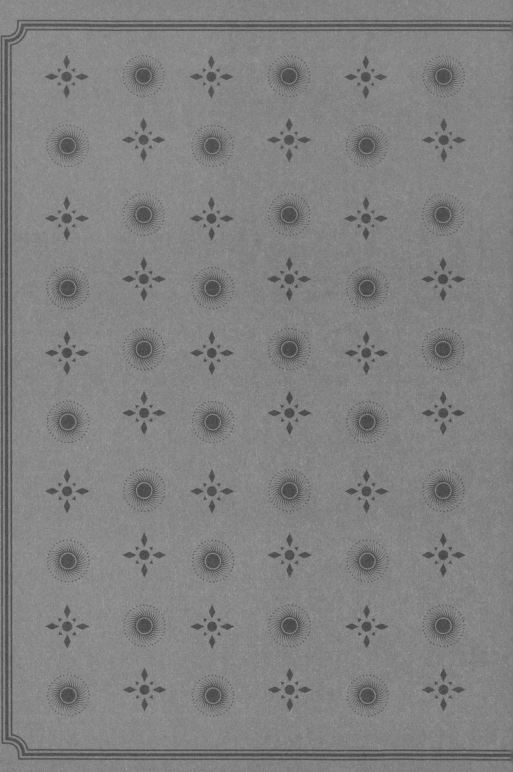

# SHARERS & PUNCHES

# GARDEN COOLER

700 ML LONDON DRY GIN

500 ML LEMON JUICE

250 ML SUGAR SYRUP

250 ML ELDERFLOWER CORDIAL

500 ML GREEN TEA, CHILLED

500 ML MINT TEA, CHILLED

500 ML APPLE JUICE

500 ML SODA WATER

PEACH, TO GARNISH

Add all the ingredients and a generous amount of ice cubes to a punch bowl and stir.

Garnish with peach slices.

# ON THE LAWN

**2 MEASURES GIN**

**2 MEASURES PIMM'S NO. 1 CUP**

**LEMONADE & GINGER ALE, TO TOP**

**STRAWBERRIES**

**ORANGES**

Fill 2 highball glasses with ice and fresh fruit such as strawberries and peeled orange segments.

Add the Pimm's No. 1 Cup and gin to each one and top up with lemonade and ginger ale.

# ENGLISH GARDEN FIZZ

**500 ML LONDON DRY GIN**

**250 ML TRIPLE SEC**

**250 ML LEMON JUICE**

**250 ML SUGAR SYRUP**

**250 ML APPLE JUICE**

**500 ML GREEN TEA, CHILLED**

**500 ML SODA WATER**

**1 BUNCH MINT LEAVES**

**CUCUMBER, TO GARNISH**

Add the gin and 1 bunch mint leaves to a large punch bowl and leave to infuse for 1 hour.

Remove the mint, add the rest of the ingredients and some ice cubes to the punch bowl.

Stir and garnish with cucumber slices.

# EARL'S PUNCH

**4 MEASURES GIN**

**6 MEASURES EARL GREY TEA, CHILLED**

**6 MEASURES PINK GRAPEFRUIT JUICE**

**6 MEASURES SODA WATER**

**1 MEASURE SUGAR SYRUP**

**PINK GRAPEFRUIT SLICES & BLACK**

**CHERRIES, TO GARNISH**

Fill a jug with ice cubes, add all the remaining ingredients and stir.

Garnish with pink grapefruit slices and black cherries.

141

# WHITE SANGRIA

**4 MEASURES VODKA**

**6 MEASURES APPLE JUICE**

**2 MEASURES LEMON JUICE**

**2 MEASURES ELDERFLOWER CORDIAL**

**6 MEASURES WHITE WINE**

**6 MEASURES SODA WATER**

**APPLE, LEMON & MINT, TO GARNISH**

Fill a jug with ice cubes, add all the remaining ingredients and stir.

Garnish with apple and lemon slices and mint leaves.

# SAKURA PUNCH

4 MEASURES VODKA

200 ML ROSÉ WINE

4 MEASURES LYCHEE JUICE

4 MEASURES PINK GRAPEFRUIT JUICE

1 MEASURE ROSE SYRUP (SEE PAGE 209)

1 MEASURE LEMON JUICE

6 MEASURES SODA WATER

TINNED LYCHEES, LEMON & MARASCHINO

CHERRIES, TO GARNISH

Fill a large jug with ice cubes, add
all the ingredients and stir.

Garnish with tinned lychees, lemon
slices and maraschino cherries.

# SPARKLING CRANBERRY PUNCH

**4 MEASURES VODKA**

**250 ML CRANBERRY JUICE COCKTAIL**

**4 MEASURES LEMONADE**

**4 MEASURES GINGER ALE**

**LEMON, LIME, CRANBERRIES & MINT**

**LEAVES, TO GARNISH**

Combine the cranberry juice, vodka and lemonade in a large jug and chill in the refrigerator for 2-3 hours.

Just before serving add the ginger ale and ice cubes.

145

# LONG ISLAND ICED TEA

**2 MEASURES VODKA**

**2 MEASURES GIN**

**2 MEASURES WHITE RUM**

**2 MEASURES TEQUILA**

**2 MEASURES COINTREAU**

**2 MEASURES LEMON JUICE**

**COLA, TO TOP**

**LEMON, TO GARNISH**

Put the vodka, gin, rum, tequila, Cointreau and lemon juice in a cocktail shaker with some ice cubes and shake to mix.

Strain into 4 highball glasses filled with ice cubes, top up with cola and garnish with lemon slices.

# LOLA'S PUNCH

**3 MEASURES WHITE RUM**

**3 MEASURES LEMON JUICE**

**3 MEASURES APPLE JUICE**

**3 MEASURES MANGO JUICE**

**3 MEASURES SUGAR SYRUP**

**4 MEASURES SODA WATER**

**PROSECCO, TO TOP**

**MANGO & APPLE, TO GARNISH**

Add all the ingredients to a jug or punch bowl filled with cubed ice and stir well.

Garnish with slices of mango and apple.

# PARISIAN FIZZ

2 MEASURES RASPBERRY PUREE

4 MEASURES PASSION FRUIT JUICE

2 MEASURES SUGAR SYRUP

1 MEASURE PERNOD

1 BOTTLE PROSECCO

RASPBERRIES & MINT, TO GARNISH

Add all the ingredients to a punch bowl filled with cubed ice and stir well.

Garnish with raspberries and sprigs of mint.

# VESPERTILLO

**4 MEASURES APEROL**

**4 PINKS PINK GRAPEFRUIT**

**2 MEASURES PASSION FRUIT SYRUP**

**1 MEASURE LEMON JUICE**

**PROSECCO, TO TOP**

**ORANGE & GRAPEFRUIT, TO GARNISH**

Add all the ingredients to a jug or punch bowl filled with cubed ice and stir well.

Garnish with slices of orange and grapefruit.

151

# BLUSH SANGRIA

**4 MEASURES VODKA**

**2 MEASURES RASPBERRY LIQUEUR**

**4 MEASURES CRANBERRY JUICE**

**2 MEASURES LIME JUICE**

**1 MEASURE SUGAR SYRUP**

**PROSECCO, TO TOP**

**EDIBLE FLOWERS, TO GARNISH**

Add all the ingredients to a jug or punch bowl filled with cubed ice and stir well.

Garnish with edible flowers.

# MULLED ORCHARD

4 MEASURES BOURBON

6 MEASURES CIDER

4 MEASURES APPLE JUICE

1 MEASURE LEMON JUICE

1 MEASURE SPICED

1 KNOB BUTTER

CINNAMON STICKS, TO GARNISH

Melt the butter in a saucepan over a gentle heat and add the apple juice, lemon juice, spiced sugar syrup, bourbon and cider. Stir until hot.

Pour carefully into a teapot and serve in heatproof glasses, garnished with cinnamon sticks.

# SOUTHERN BELLE

**6 MEASURES BOURBON**

**200 ML CIDER**

**2 MEASURE LEMON JUICE**

**2 MEASURES APPLE JUICE**

**4 MEASURE YELLOW TEA**

**2 MEASURES SUGAR SYRUP**

**APPLE & LEMON, TO GARNISH**


Fill a large jug with ice cubes, add
6 measures bourbon, 2 measures
lemon juice, 2 measures sugar syrup,
4 measures yellow tea, 2 measures
apple juice and 200 ml cider and stir.

Garnish with apple and lemon slices.

# BATON BLANC

**2 MEASURE BOURBON**

**200 ML WHEAT BEER**

**2 MEASURES LEMON JUICE**

**2 MEASURES ORANGE JUICE**

**2 MEASURES SUGAR SYRUP**

**2 TSP MARMALADE**

**ORANGE, TO GARNISH**

Put 4 measures bourbon, 2 measures lemon juice, 2 measures orange juice, 2 measures sugar syrup and 2 teaspoons marmalade in a food processor or blender and blend until smooth.

Pour into a large jug, add 200 ml wheat beer and top up the jug with ice cubes.

Garnish with orange wheels to serve.

157

# BLUE GRASS PUNCH

**4 MEASURES BOURBON**

**3 TSP MARMALADE**

**2 MEASURES LEMON JUICE**

**1 MEASURE SUGAR SYRUP**

**2 MEASURES CRANBERRY JUICE**

**6 MEASURES SODA WATER**

**DRIED ORANGE WHEELS, TO GARNISH**

Add the bourbon and marmalade to a jug and stir until dissolved.

Add all the remaining ingredients and fill the jug with ice cubes. Stir.

Garnish with dried orange wheels to serve.

# PLANTER'S PUNCH

**4 MEASURES MYER'S JAMAICAN PLANTER'S**

**PUNCH RUM**

**8 DROPS ANGOSTURA BITTERS**

**1 MEASURE LIME JUICE**

**4 MEASURES CHILLED WATER**

**2 MEASURES SUGAR SYRUP**

**ORANGE & LIME, TO GARNISH**

Put the rum, bitters, lime juice, water and sugar syrup in a cocktail shaker and add some ice cubes.

Shake and strain into 2 chilled glasses and garnish with orange and lime slices.

# RUM PUNCH

**200 ML SPICED RUM**

**4 MEASURES LIME JUICE**

**4 MEASURES SUGAR SYRUP**

**6 MEASURES PASSION FRUIT JUICE**

**6 MEASURES PINEAPPLE JUICE**

**6 MEASURES ORANGE JUICE**

**ORANGE, LIME & PASSION FRUIT, TO GARNISH**

Fill a large jug with ice cubes, add all the ingredients and stir.

Garnish with orange and lime slices and passion fruit halves.

161

# PIÑA COCO

**4 MEASURES AMBER RUM**

**1 MEASURE GALLIANO**

**1 MEASURE COCONUT CREAM**

**4 MEASURES PASSION FRUIT JUICE**

**1 PINEAPPLE**

**1 BANANA**

Cut the top off the pineapple and use a pineapple corer to remove the flesh inside the pineapple. Set aside the hollowed-out pineapple.

Cut the pineapple flesh into chunks.

Add 7 chunks of the pineapple and the remaining ingredients to a food processor or blender and blend until smooth.

Pour into the hollowed-out pineapple and serve with straws.

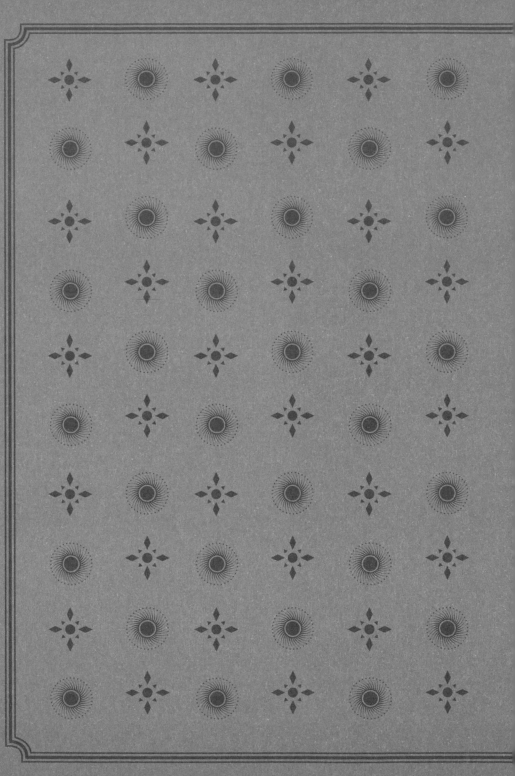

CLASSICS

# NEGRONI

**1 MEASURE GIN**

**1 MEASURE SWEET VERMOUTH**

**1 MEASURE CAMPARI**

**ORANGE, TO GARNISH**

Fill a glass with ice cubes, add all the ingredients and stir.

Garnish with an orange wedge.

# CLOVER CLUB

**2 MEASURES GIN**

**¾ MEASURE LEMON JUICE**

**¾ MEASURE SUGAR SYRUP**

**5 RASPBERRIES**

**½ MEASURE EGG WHITE**

**RASPBERRIES, TO GARNISH**

Add all the ingredients to your cocktail shaker and dry shake without ice for 10 seconds.

Take the shaker apart, add cubed ice and shake vigorously.

Strain into a cocktail glass and garnish with raspberries.

# VESPER MARTINI

**2 ½ MEASURES GIN**

**1 MEASURE VODKA**

**½ MEASURE LILLET BLANC WINE**

**LEMON, TO GARNISH**

Add all the ingredients into the bottom of your cocktail shaker, and fill the top half of it with ice.

Shake vigorously and double strain into a chilled martini glass.

Garnish with a lemon twist.

# CLASSIC MARTINI

**6 MEASURES GIN**

**1 MEASURE DRY VERMOUTH**

**STUFFED GREEN OLIVES, TO GARNISH**

Put 10–12 ice cubes into a mixing glass.

Pour over the vermouth and gin and stir (never shake) vigorously and evenly without splashing.

Strain into 2 chilled martini glasses, garnish each with a green olive.

# AVIATION

**2 MEASURES GIN**

**½ MEASURES MARASCHINO LIQUEUR**

**½ MEASURES LEMON JUICE**

**COCKTAIL CHERRY, TO GARNISH**

Put some ice cubes into a cocktail shaker with the gin, maraschino liqueur and lemon juice.

Shake well and double strain into a chilled martini glass.

Garnish with a cocktail cherry on a cocktail stick.

# GIMLET

**2 ½ MEASURES GIN**

**½ MEASURE LIME CORDIAL**

**½ MEASURE LIME JUICE**

**LIME, TO GARNISH**

Add all the ingredients to your cocktail shaker, shake and strain into a chilled cocktail glass.

Garnish with a lime rind spiral.

# TOM COLLINS

**2 MEASURES GIN**

**1 MEASURE LEMON JUICE**

**1 MEASURE SUGAR SYRUP**

**4 MEASURES SODA WATER**

**LEMON & BLACK CHERRY, TO GARNISH**

Put all the ingredients except the soda water into cocktail shaker and fill with ice cubes.

Shake then strain into a glass full of ice cubes and top up with the soda water.

Garnish with a lemon wedge and a black cherry.

# SCREWDRIVER

**1½ MEASURES VODKA**

**ORANGE JUICE, TO TOP**

**ORANGE, TO GARNISH**

Put some ice cubes into a tumbler and pour the vodka over them.

Top up with orange juice and stir lightly.

Garnish with orange slice quarters and serve with a straw.

# MOSCOW MULE

**2 MEASURES VODKA**

**JUICE OF 2 LIMES**

**GINGER BEER, TO TOP**

Put 6–8 cracked ice cubes in a cocktail shaker, add 4 measures vodka and the juice of 4 limes and shake well.

Pour, without straining, into a highball glass over ice and top up with ginger beer.

# COSMOPOLITAN

**1½ MEASURES LEMON VODKA**

**4 TSP TRIPLE SEC**

**3 TSP LIME JUICE**

**1 MEASURE CRANBERRY JUICE**

**LIME, TO GARNISH**

Add all the ingredients to a cocktail shaker and shake and strain into a glass.

Garnish with a lime wedge.

# SCREWDRIVER

**1 MEASURE VODKA**

**1 MEASURE TIA MARIA**

**1 MEASURE MILK OR DOUBLE CREAM**

Put 3 cracked ice cubes into
a cocktail shaker and add the
vodka, Tia Maria and milk or cream.

Shake until a frost forms.

Strain into a tall, narrow glass over
a few more cracked ice cubes.

# BLOODY MARY

**JUICE OF ½ LEMON**

**½ TSP HORSERADISH SAUCE**

**2 DROPS WORCESTERSHIRE SAUCE**

**1 DROP TABASCO SAUCE**

**2 MEASURES THICK TOMATO JUICE**

**2 MEASURES VODKA**

**PINCH OF SALT**

**PINCH OF CAYENNE PEPPER**

**LEMON, GREEN OLIVES, CELERY STICK,**

**WITH THE LEAVES LEFT ON, TO GARNISH**

Put some ice cubes into a cocktail shaker and pour the lemon juice, horseradish, Worcestershire and Tabasco sauces, tomato juice and vodka over the ice.

Shake until a frost forms.

Pour into a tall glass, add the salt and cayenne pepper and garnish with a celery stick, lemon slice and 3 olives.

# BELLINI

½ RIPE WHITE PEACH

1 DASH SUGAR SYRUP

PROSECCO, TO TOP

Add the peach and sugar syrup to a blender or food processor and blend until smooth.

Pour into a Champagne flute and top with chilled Prosecco.

# FRENCH 75

**1 MEASURE GIN**

**½ MEASURE LEMON JUICE**

**½ MEASURE SUGAR SYRUP**

**PROSECCO, TO TOP**

**LEMON, TO GARNISH**

Shake the gin, lemon juice and sugar syrup vigorously and strain into a Champagne flute.

Top with chilled Prosecco and garnish with a lemon twist.

# THE CLASSIC'S
# CLASSIC

**1 MEASURE GRAND MARNIER**

**1 SUGAR CUBE**

**3-4 DASHES ANGOSTURA BITTERS**

**PROSECCO, TO TOP**

**LEMON, TO FINISH**

On a clean surface, coat the sugar cube in the Angostura bitters then drop it into a Champagne flute.

Add the Grand Marnier and gently top with chilled Prosecco.

To finish, spray the oils of a lemon twist over the top of the drink, then discard it.

*185*

# SBAGLIATO

**1 MEASURE CAMPARI**

**1 MEASURE SWEET VERMOUTH**

**2 MEASURES PROSECCO**

**ORANGE, TO GARNISH**

Add the ingredients to a rocks glass filled with cubed ice, stir briefly and garnish with a slice of orange.

# OLD FASHIONED

**2 MEASURES BOURBON**

**1 TSP SUGAR SYRUP**

**1 DASH ORANGE BITTERS**

**1 DASH ANGOSTURA BITTERS**

**ORANGE, TO GARNISH**

Half-fill a glass with ice cubes.
Add the remaining ingredients to
the glass and stir for 1 minute.

Fill the glass with more ice cubes
and garnish with an orange twist.

# ROB ROY

**1 MEASURE SCOTCH WHISKY**

**½ MEASURE VERMOUTH**

**1 DASH ANGOSTURA BITTERS**

**LEMON, TO GARNISH**

Put a cracked ice cube, whisky, vermouth and bitters into a mixing glass and stir well.

Strain into a cocktail glass and garnish the rim with a lemon rind spiral.

# SAZERAC

**2 ½ MEASURES RYE WHISKEY**

**2 DASHES PEYCHAUD'S BITTERS**

**1 DASH ANGOSTURA BITTERS**

**1 DASH ABSINTHE**

**1 SUGAR CUBE**

**1 DASH WATER**

**LEMON, TO GARNISH**

Chill an old-fashioned glass or small tumbler in your freezer.

In a mixing glass, combine the sugar cube, Peychaud's Bitters, and a few drops of water. Mix until sugar is dissolved and add the whiskey. Add plenty of ice, and stir for another 30 seconds.

Pour the absinthe into your chilled glass, and rotate glass until the inside is well coated; discard the excess.

Strain the liquid from your mixing glass into the serving glass and twist a piece of lemon peel over the drink, to garnish.

# MANHATTAN

**1 MEASURE SWEET VERMOUTH**

**3 MEASURES RYE WHISKEY OR BOURBON**

**COCKTAIL CHERRY, TO GARNISH (OPTIONAL)**

Put 4–5 ice cubes into a mixing glass.

Pour the vermouth and whiskey over the ice.

Stir vigorously, then strain into a chilled cocktail glass and drop in a cocktail cherry, if you like.

# WHISKY SOUR

**2 MEASURES SCOTCH WHISKY**

**1 MEASURE LEMON JUICE**

**1 MEASURE SUGAR SYRUP**

**LEMON, TO GARNISH**

Fill a cocktail shaker with ice cubes.

Add all the ingredients and shake.

Strain into a glass filled with ice cubes and garnish with a lemon wedge and a lemon rind spiral.

# IRISH COFFEE

**1½ MEASURES IRISH WHISKEY**

**½ MEASURE COFFEE LIQUEUR**

**1 MEASURE VANILLA SYRUP**

**2 MEASURES ESPRESSO**

**WHIPPED CREAM, TO TOP**

Add all the ingredients, except the cream, to a small saucepan and gently heat till warm, but not boiling.

Pour into a rocks glass and top with whipped cream.

# DAIQUIRI

**2 MEASURES LIGHT RUM**

**1 MEASURE SUGAR SYRUP**

**1 MEASURE LIME JUICE**

**LIME, TO GARNISH**

Add all the ingredients, plus some ice cubes, to a cocktail shaker.

Shake and strain into a glass and garnish with a lime wedge.

# PIÑA COLADA

**1 MEASURE WHITE RUM**

**2 MEASURES COCONUT MILK**

**2 MEASURES PINEAPPLE JUICE**

**PINEAPPLE, TO GARNISH**

Put some cracked ice into a cocktail shaker, with the rum, coconut milk and pineapple juice.

Shake lightly to mix and strain into a large glass and garnish with the pineapple wedge.

Serve with long straws.

*198*

# ZOMBIE

1 MEASURE DARK RUM

1 MEASURE WHITE RUM

½ MEASURE GOLDEN RUM

2 TSP OVER-PROOF RUM

½ MEASURE APRICOT BRANDY

JUICE OF ½ LIME

1 TSP GRENADINE

2 MEASURES PINEAPPLE JUICE

½ MEASURE SUGAR SYRUP

PINEAPPLE WEDGE & LEAF & SUGAR, TO GARNISH

Put some ice cubes into a cocktail shaker with the dark, white and golden rums, apricot brandy, lime juice, grenadine, pineapple juice and sugar syrup and shake well.

Pour without straining into a chilled glass and float the over-proof rum on top.

Garnish with a pineapple wedge and leaf, and sprinkle a pinch of sugar over the top.

# EGG NOG

**2 MEASURES RUM**

**6 MEASURES MILK**

**1 EGG**

**1 TBSP SUGAR SYRUP**

**NUTMEG & CINNAMON STICK, TO GARNISH**

Half-fill a cocktail shaker with ice cubes. Add the egg, sugar syrup, rum and milk and shakc well for about 1 minute.

Strain into a tumbler and sprinkle with a little grated nutmeg and garnish with a cinnamon stick.

# MAI TAI

**2 MEASURES GOLDEN RUM**

**2 TSP WOOD'S NAVY RUM**

**½ MEASURE ORANGE CURAÇAO**

**½ MEASURE ORGEAT SYRUP**

**JUICE OF 1 LIME**

**LIME & MINT SPRIG, TO GARNISH**

Put some ice cubes into a cocktail shaker with the golden rum, Curaçao, orgeat syrup and lime juice and shake well.

Strain over crushed ice into an old-fashioned glass, float the Navy rum on top and garnish with lime rind and a mint sprig.

# HURRICANE

**1 MEASURE WHITE RUM**

**1 MEASURE GOLDEN RUM**

**2 TSP PASSION FRUIT SYRUP**

**2 TSP LIME JUICE**

Put some ice cubes into a cocktail shaker and pour over the rums, passion fruit syrup and lime juice.

Shake well and strain into a cocktail glass and add ice cubes.

# MOJITO

**5 MEASURES WHITE RUM**

**16 MINT LEAVES, PLUS SPRIGS, TO GARNISH**

**1 LIME, CUT INTO WEDGES**

**4 TSP CANE SUGAR**

**SODA WATER, TO TOP**

Muddle the mint leaves, lime and sugar in the bottom of 2 highball glasses and fill with crushed ice.

Add the rum, stir and top up with soda water.

Garnish with mint sprigs and serve with straws.

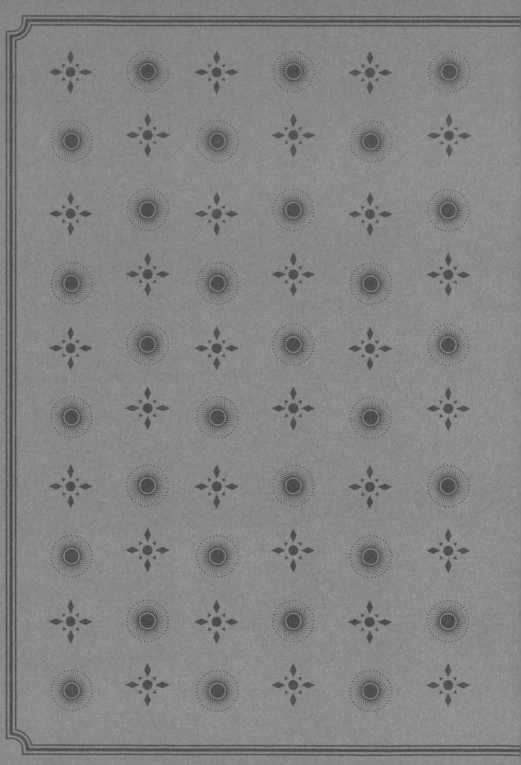

# TIPS & TECHNIQUES FOR CRAFTING THE PERFECT COCKTAIL

# WHAT MAKES A GOOD COCKTAIL?

Good cocktails, like good food, are based around quality ingredients. As with cooking, using fresh and homemade ingredients can often make the huge difference between a good drink and an outstanding drink. All of this can be found in department stores, online or in kitchen shops.

## COCKTAIL INGREDIENTS

**ICE** This is a key part of cocktails and you'll need lots of it. Purchase it from your supermarket or freeze big tubs of water, then crack this up to use in your drinks. If you're hosting a big party and want to serve some punches, which will need lots of ice, it may be worthwhile finding if you have a local ice supplier that supplies catering companies, as this can be much more cost effective.

**CITRUS JUICE** It's important to use fresh citrus juice in your drinks; bottled versions taste awful and will not produce good drinks. Store your fruit out of the refrigerator at room temperature. Look for a soft-skinned fruit for juicing, which you can do with a juicer or citrus press. You can keep fresh citrus juice for a couple of days in the refrigerator, sealed to prevent oxidation.

**SUGAR SYRUP**  You can buy sugar syrup or you can make your own. The most basic form of sugar syrup is made by mixing caster sugar and hot water together, and stirring until the sugar has dissolved. The key when preparing sugar syrups is to use a 1:1 ratio of sugar to liquid. White sugar acts as a flavour enhancer, while dark sugars have unique, more toffee flavours and work well with dark spirits.

**BASIC SUGAR SYRUP RECIPE**
(Makes 1 litre) Dissolve 1 kg caster sugar in 1 litre of hot water. Allow to cool.
Sugar syrup will keep in a sterilized bottle stored in the refrigerator for up to 2 weeks.

**ROSE SYRUP**  Follow same method as above with the addition of 25 ml rose essence when dissolving the sugar.

**ORANGE & CHERRY-INFUSED BOURBON**
Muddle 6 slices orange and 6 glacier cherries in a jar and add 500 ml bourbon. Steep for 24 hours before straining. Follow same method for lemon or orange-infused bourbon.

**LEMON GRASS-INFUSED VODKA**  Add 4–5 chopped shoots of lemon grass to 500 ml vodka and leave to infuse for 24 hours.

# CHOOSING GLASSWARE

There are many different cocktails, but they all fall into one of three categories: long, short or shot. Long drinks generally have more mixer than alcohol, often served with ice and a straw. The terms 'straight up' and 'on the rocks' are synonymous with the short drink, which tends to be more about the spirit, often combined with a single mixer at most. Finally, there is the shot which is made up mainly from spirits and liqueurs, designed to give a quick hit of alcohol. Glasses are tailored to the type of drinks they will contain.

**CHAMPAGNE FLUTE**   Used for Champagne or Champagne cocktails, the narrow mouth of the flute helps the drink to stay fizzy.

**CHAMPAGNE SAUCER**   A classic glass, but not very practical for serving Champagne as the drink quickly loses its fizz.

**MARGARITA OR COUPETTE GLASS**   When used for a Margarita, the rim is dipped in salt. Also used for daiquiris and other fruit-based cocktails.

**HIGHBALL GLASS**   Suitable for any long cocktail, such as a Long Island Iced Tea.

**COLLINS GLASS**  This is similar to a highball glass but is slightly narrower.

**WINE GLASS**  Sangria is often served in one, but they are not usually used for cocktails.

**OLD-FASHIONED GLASS**  Also known as a rocks glass, this is great for any drink that's served on the rocks or straight up.

**SHOT GLASS**  Often found in two sizes — for a single or double measure. They are ideal for a single mouthful.

**BALLOON GLASS**  Often used for fine spirits. The glass can be warmed to encourage the release of the drink's aroma.

**HURRICANE GLASS**  Mostly found in beach bars, used for creamy, rum-based drinks.

**BOSTON GLASS**  Often used by bartenders for mixing cocktails, good for fruity drinks.

**TODDY GLASS**  A toddy glass is generally used for a hot drink, such as Irish Coffee.

**SLING GLASS**  This has a very short stemmed base and is most famously used for a Singapore Sling.

**MARTINI GLASS**  Also known as a cocktail glass, its thin neck design makes sure your hand can't warm the glass, or the cocktail.

# USEFUL EQUIPMENT

Some pieces of equipment, such as shakers and the correct glasses, are vital for any cocktail party, while others, like ice buckets, can be obtained at a later date if needed. Below is a wishlist for anyone who wants to make cocktails on a regular basis.

**SHAKER**  The Boston shaker is the most simple option, but it needs to be used in conjunction with a hawthorne strainer. Alternatively you could choose a shaker with a built-in strainer.

**MEASURE OR JIGGER**  Single and double measures are available and are essential when you are mixing ingredients so that the proportions are always the same. One measure is 25 ml or 1 fl oz.

**MIXING GLASS**  A mixing glass is used for those drinks that require only a gentle stirring before they are poured or strained.

**HAWTHORNE STRAINER**  This type of strainer is often used in conjunction with a Boston shaker, but a simple tea strainer will also work well.

**BAR SPOON**  Similar to a teaspoon but with a long handle, a bar spoon is used for stirring, layering and muddling drinks.

**MUDDLING STICK**  Similar to a pestle, which will work just as well, a muddling stick, or muddler, is used to crush fruit or herbs in a glass or shaker for drinks like the Mojito.

**BOTTLE OPENER**  Choose a bottle opener with two attachments, one for metal-topped bottles and a corkscrew for wine bottles.

**POURERS**  A pourer is inserted into the top of a spirit bottle to enable the spirit to flow in a controlled manner.

**FOOD PROCESSOR**  A food processor or blender is useful for making frozen cocktails and smoothies.

**EQUIPMENT FOR GARNISHING**  Many drinks are garnished with fruit on cocktail sticks and these are available in wood, plastic or glass. Exotic drinks may be prettified with a paper umbrella and several long drinks are served with straws or swizzle sticks.

# TECHNIQUES

With just a few basic techniques, your bartending skills will be complete. Follow the instructions to hone your craft.

**BLENDING**   Frozen cocktails and smoothies are blended with ice in a blender until they are of a smooth consistency. Be careful not to add too much ice as this will dilute the cocktail. It's best to add a little at a time.

**SHAKING**   The best-known cocktail technique and probably the most common. Used to mix ingredients thoroughly and quickly, and to chill the drink before serving.
**1** Half-fill a cocktail shaker with ice cubes, or cracked or crushed ice.
**2** If the recipe calls for a chilled glass add a few ice cubes and some cold water to the glass, swirl it around and discard.
**3** Add the ingredients to the shaker and shake until a frost forms on the outside.
**4** Strain the cocktail into the glass and serve.

**MUDDLING**   A technique used to bring out the flavours of herbs and fruit using a blunt tool called a muddler.
**1** Add chosen herb(s) to a highball glass. Add some sugar syrup and some lime wedges.
**2** Hold the glass firmly and use a muddler or pestle to twist and press down.

**3** Continue for 30 seconds, top up with crushed ice and add remaining ingredients.

**DOUBLE-STRAINING**  To prevent all traces of puréed fruit and ice fragments from entering the glass, use a shaker with a built-in strainer in conjunction with a hawthorne strainer. A fine strainer also works well.

**LAYERING**  Some spirits can be served layered on top of each other, causing 'lighter' spirits to float on top of your cocktail.
**1** Pour the first ingredient into a glass, taking care that it does not touch the sides.
**2** Position a bar spoon in the centre of the glass, rounded part down and facing you. Rest the spoon against the side of the glass as your pour the second ingredient down the spoon. It should float on top of the first liquid.
**3** Repeat with the third ingredient, then carefully remove the spoon.

**STIRRING**  Used when the ingredients need to be mixed and chilled, but also maintain their clarity. This ensures there are no ice fragments or air bubbles throughout the drink. Some cocktails require the ingredients to be prepared in a mixing glass, then strained into the serving glass.
**1** Add ingredients to a glass, in recipe order.
**2** Use a bar spoon to stir the drink, lightly or vigorously, as described in the recipe.
**3** Finish the drink with any decoration and serve.

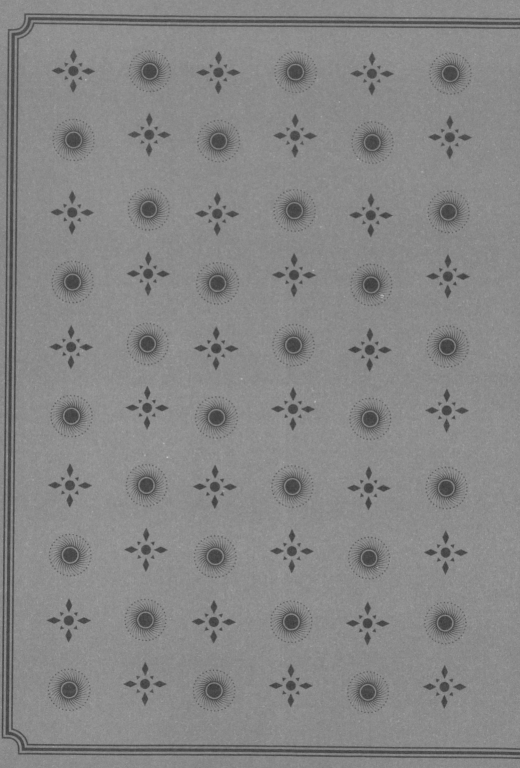

# INDEX

*221*

# PICTURE CREDITS